LONG AGO and TODAY

A Home Album

Peter and Connie Roop

Heinemann Library
Des Plaines, Illinois

© 1999 Reed Educational & Professional Publishing
Published by Heinemann Library,
an imprint of Reed Educational & Professional Publishing,
1350 East Touhy Avenue, Suite 240 West
Des Plaines, IL 60018

Designed by Lindaanne Donohoe
Printed in Hong Kong

03 02 01 00 99
10 9 8 7 6 5 4 3 2 1

Library of Congress Cataloging-in-Publication Data
Roop, Peter
    A home album / Peter and Connie Roop.
        p.   cm. — (Long ago and today)
    Includes bibliographical references and index.
    Summary: Text, photographs, and illustrations identify and trace
patterns of continuity and change in homes and home life in the
United States, including such topics as types of homes, house work,
playing, bathing, sleeping, and more.
    ISBN 1-57572-602-5 (lib. bdg.)
    1. Family—United States—History—Juvenile literature. 2. Home
-United States—History—Juvenile literature. 3. United States
—Social life and customs—Juvenile literature. (1. Home.
2. Dwellings. 3. United States—Social life and customs.)
I. Roop, Connie. II. Title. III. Series: Roop, Peter. Long ago
and today.
HQ535.R63 1998
306.85'0973—dc21   98-17900
                                                                    CIP
                                                                    AC

Acknowledgments
The authors and publishers are grateful to the following for permission to reproduce
copyright photographs:
Cover photographs: Stock Montage, Inc. top, and Steve Benbow, bottom
Corbis-Bettmann, pp. 4, 6, 16; Stock Montage, Inc., pp.10, 12, 14; Culver Pictures, pp. 18, 20
back cover; Steve Benbow, p. 13; Phil Martin, pp. 5, 7, 8, 9, 11, 15, 17, 19, 21; Old World
Wisconsin, p. 22 top and bottom.

Every effort has been made to contact copyright holders of any material reproduced in this
book. Any omissions will be rectified in subsequent printings if notice is given to the publisher.

Some words are shown in bold, **like this.** You can find out what they mean by looking
in the glossary.

Especially for Joan—Thank you for your caring attitude and friendship.
You make everyone feel at home!

Contents

The Home. 4

Kinds of Homes 6

Food and Water. 8

Cooking. 10

Chores 12

Playing. .14

Laundry .16

Bathing .18

Sleeping 20

Homes Long Ago and Today. 22

Glossary 23

More Books to Read 23

Index. 24

The Home

a one-room log cabin, 1896

A long time ago, families lived in different kinds of homes. Families worked, did **chores,** ate, and slept in their homes. They played in and around their homes.

Today, families also live in many different kinds of homes. Families eat, sleep, play, and do chores at home. Children today do many of the same things children did long ago, but they do them in different ways.

single family home with built-in garage, 1998

Kinds of Homes

Long ago, **pioneer** children lived in log cabins in the woods. Other children lived in wood houses in **villages.** Children in cities lived in wood or brick houses. Most houses were small.

home above a store in New York City, 1885

a row of houses on a city street, 1998

Today, many people live in apartment buildings.
Some families live in houses on a farm or in the
country. Many people live in houses on blocks
in cities and towns.

Food and Water

*Drinking water was carried from a stream or pumped from a **well**.*

Long ago, people grew most of their own food in a garden near the house. Families grew vegetables to eat. Fruit came from **orchards.** They got milk and meat from animals.

Today, people buy most of their food. They buy vegetables, fruit, and meat at a grocery store or supermarket. Some people grow food in gardens.

Drinking water is piped to homes and comes out a faucet.

Cooking

The fireplace or stove also warmed the house in winter.

Long ago, people cooked food in fireplaces or on stoves that burned wood. Big pots held the cooking food. Bread was baked in fireplaces or stove ovens. Dishes were washed by hand.

Today, people cook food on stoves, ovens, and in microwaves run by gas or electricity. Many homes are heated with a **furnace** that burns oil or gas. Other homes have heating and cooling machines.

Dishes are washed in the sink or in a dishwasher.

Chores

Long ago, children did many **chores** each day. Children milked cows or goats. They chopped firewood for cooking and heating. Others took care of younger brothers and sisters.

Some children fed chickens or weeded the garden.

Many children today take care of pets.

Today, children do many jobs around the home. Farm children help take care of animals. Some work in their family's garden. Some take care of younger children. Children also help do the dishes, empty the garbage, and clean.

Playing

playing at a playground in Chicago, Illinois, 1890

Long ago, people played after their work was done. Children played in playgrounds. They jumped rope or played marbles or checkers. They swam in lakes or ponds. Many children made their own toys from wood or cloth. Many listened to adults tell stories.

Today, people play, too. Children go to playgrounds to swing or play games. They play in their yards. They play sports or take music or dance lessons. They ride bikes and skate on roller blades. Today, most toys and games are bought in stores. Many people watch television or play video games. Children still listen to stories read aloud.

playing on a jungle gym, Wilton, North Dakota, 1998

Laundry

Long ago, people did not have very many clothes. Keeping clothes clean was hard work. Soap had to be made. Water had to be carried to a washtub. Wet clothes were hung up to dry.

Clothes had to be scrubbed by hand.

Many families dry wet clothes in a hot dryer.

Today, people have many kinds of clothes. People buy soap to wash their clothes. Clothes are washed in a washing machine at home or in a **laundromat.** Some people still hang their clothes up to dry.

Bathing

Children often shared the same bath water.

Long ago, people bathed only once a week. Water was carried to the kitchen, heated, and then put in a tub. Children were scrubbed with homemade soap.

Today, people bathe more than once a week.
They bathe in tubs and showers in their homes.
Hot water is heated by a water heater and
comes rushing out of a faucet.

Bubble bath soap is used in many baths today.

Sleeping

Children often had to share the same bed.

Long ago, people slept in beds or on the floor. Beds were made from wood with ropes to hold up a mattress. Mattresses were stuffed with **corn husks** or feathers. Pillows were stuffed with feathers, too. Few children had their own bedrooms.

Today, many children sleep in their own bedrooms or share a room with a brother or sister. Few people share beds. Beds are made of wood or metal. Mattresses are made of cloth. Pillows are stuffed with feathers or foam rubber.

Some children sleep in bunkbeds today.

Homes Long Ago and Today

Today, we can visit old homes to see how people lived long ago. We can see how people cooked, cleaned, played, and slept. We can see that people who lived long ago did the same things we do but they did them in different ways.

Glossary

chores jobs

corn husks dry, outer covering of corn

furnace machine that heats homes and other buildings

laundromat place with washing and drying machines where people do their laundry

orchards large group of trees grown for their fruit

pioneer first people to live in a new country or area

villages very small towns

well deep hole in the ground where water is brought out

More Books to Read

Desimin, Lisa. *My House.* New York: Henry Holt & Company, 1994.

Grimshaw, Caroline. *Our Homes.* Chicago: World Book, 1998.

Morgan, Sally. *Homes & Cities: Living for the Future.* New York: Franklin Watts, 1998.

Rounds, Glen. *Sod Houses on the Great Plains.* New York: Holiday House, 1995.

Steele, Philip. *House Through the Ages.* Mahwah, NJ: Troll Communications, 1993.

Index

animals 8, 12, 13

apartments 7

bathing 18–19

beds 20–21

chores 4, 5, 12–13

clothes dryer 17

cooking 10–11, 12, 22

dishes 10, 11, 13

electricity 11

farms 7

fireplace 10

firewood 12

food 8–9

furnace 11

gardens 8, 9, 12

gas 11

laundry 16–17

microwaves 11

orchards 8

ovens 11

pets 13

pillows 20, 21

pioneer 6

playgrounds 14–15

playing 4, 5, 14–15, 22

sleeping 20–21, 22

soap 16, 17, 18

stoves 10

toys 14–15

villages 6

water 8–9, 16, 17, 18, 19